Light for the World

Praying the new mysteries of the Rosary

Greg Crowhurst

kevin mayhew

For my Linda: dancing spirit

I would like to acknowledge the crucial support of Marisa Dunkley, my wife's prayer partner, Mary Fuller and Anna Heathfield whose love and prayers more than make up for the isolation.

Published in 2004 by
KEVIN MAYHEW LTD
Buxhall, Stowmarket, Suffolk, IP14 3BW
E-mail: info@kevinmayhewltd.com

9 8 7 6 5 4 3 2 1 0

ISBN 1 84417 342 9
Catalogue No. 1500747

Cover design by Angela Selfe
Edited by Marian Reid
Typesetting by Richard Weaver

Printed and bound in Great Britain

Contents

'I am the Light of the World.'
John 9:5

I look to all of you, brothers and sisters of every state of life, to you, Christian families, to you the sick and the elderly, and to you, young people: confidently take up the Rosary once again. Rediscover the Rosary in the light of Scripture, in harmony with the Liturgy, and the context of your daily lives.

Apostolic Letter of the Supreme Pontiff Pope John Paul II to the Bishops, Clergy and Faithful, *Rosarium Virginis Mariae*, on the most holy Rosary, 16 October 2002

Preface

My wife Linda, chronically ill, disabled, and virtually bed-bound, has known nothing but intense physical pain on every level, every moment, for the last ten years. Yet through it all, she has meditated continually on God's light – it is what keeps her centred, keeps her going. When the Mysteries of Light were introduced by Pope John Paul II, she was ecstatic. Hardly able to contain her excitement, she could immediately point out the connections, the flow of light, the power of the Holy Spirit, centred upon us and lifting us all up into the Trinity.

What follows is more than words, for each word is suffused – sparkles, it seems to me – with dancing light. It has been a joy to collect together the meditations and thoughts of Linda, which in turn have inspired my own contemplation and writing.

Just after his election to the Papacy, the Holy Father dedicated his whole ministry to the prophetic role that the sick and disabled play in the life of the Church. He also revealed that the Rosary has always been his favourite prayer. This work significantly brings both of those strands together.

Introduction to the Mysteries of Light

On 16 October 2002, John Paul II introduced a new addition to the Rosary. The Pope calls these mysteries the 'Mysteries of Light' because Christ in his public life manifests himself as 'the mystery of light' (John 9:5).

The Rosary has been with us since the fourteenth century, and has been well prayed and loved ever since, largely untouched in its original form. The impact of adding a whole new section addressing the adult ministry of Jesus is a ground-breaking event and its potential impact cannot be understated.

This book is a signpost. Words can only be pointers to the Light, which must be contemplated and pondered, alongside Mary, in the silence and depths of the heart. The Love of the Father, the Truth of the Son and the Power of the Holy Spirit work in unity, and are the very essence of the Mysteries of Light. God's love and mercy are so powerfully illuminated in this wonderful new addition to the Rosary.

In today's world, where there is an emphasis upon New Age spirituality and talk of spiritual light, the Mysteries of Light bring a much-needed focus. For they offer sound guidance and a safe passage for those seeking the Truth. The only true light of the world is Christ himself; our saviour and our salvation.

Seeing the mysteries unfold before our eyes helps us to see more clearly that Jesus is the Light of the world. Contemplating each mystery helps us to experience this Light and receive its blessings: for experience it we must.

There are no words to articulate this experience fully. The mind just cannot describe, cannot record such moments. But almost mischievously, tenderly, the soul speaks. It is too wild for words, too passionate for analysis, so, bubbling and churning in the poetry of the psalms, the eroticism of the Song of Songs, the mysticism of John, the soul speaks in the language of light. How then can we speak about the Mysteries of Light, if not as the bride speaks to the bridegroom, as lover to beloved?

May I suggest that you approach these mysteries with new eyes, seeking new things, reaching out tenderly, gently and hopefully – for, just as the bride needs to learn, to grow in confidence, to believe and to trust in something greater, so, too, do we need to learn and grow in confidence, to believe and trust in something greater still.

And that is the wonder of love.

Praying the New Mysteries of Light

Let us seek the Light – for it is always there. Look upwards, rise up to the Light, transcend all troubles, fear, worries and anxieties. Be filled with the peace and love of God – for here anything is possible.

Filled with Holy Light, we will lead powerful lives of oneness and wonder. For Christ is the Light and all things are held and healed in him.

He is with us.

To choose Life is to consciously choose to live in the light of the Father, Son and Holy Spirit. Could we say no? Could we choose another way?

We desperately need to live in Light.

A wonderful gift has been given to us. Through the intercession of Mary, the Mother of God, let us pray the Mysteries of Light.

Understanding the Mysteries

The rosary has a peaceful effect on all who pray it, because it leads us to see 'the face of Christ', says the Holy Father.

To look upon Christ's face is to look upon compassion and tenderness, all wisdom, all knowledge, all love. It is to approach the truth of the mystery of love and to be blessed with the most astonishing gift.

If we dare to look into the eyes of Christ, we will see that he is here and we are loved absolutely, unconditionally. We will see the face of mercy and know that forgiveness is possible – and not only that, but that all forgiveness is here. As we gaze in awe and wonder we will be led to the most precious gift, we will begin to see and come to know the Father who is so intimately bound with the Son, and we will come to feel the power of their love and be filled with the utter joy of the Holy Spirit who is the messenger of love and who resides with them in oneness.

Stop, says the Pope, and look at the crucifix on your rosary. 'The life and prayer of believers is centred upon Christ; everything begins from him, everything leads toward him, everything through him, in the Holy Spirit, attains to the Father.'

As we come to look and learn and grow in love of the Trinity, we will be filled with hope and lifted to new levels of joy, for we, too, will be joined in oneness – and nothing will be the same again.

The key to understanding the Mysteries of Light is Christ's *light*:

Light

Illuminating

God's

Holy

Truth

We need, says Pope John Paul II, to allow God to 'speak' to us in the rosary. In a very special way in these new mysteries, we look to where the light is shining, in order to discover what it is God wants us to see. It will always be something new, something not visible before Christ's life in the world, which is illuminated.

What does light do? It shows us something not previously visible. The pure white light of Christ is so bright that it can even dazzle. Peace and joy, pure love, radiates from this light, helping us to know God's word more truly.

The Light always illuminates truth; as we find Christ through seeking him, we will know more truly how to serve God, because we will live in his presence with greater awareness.

As we enter into the Mysteries of Light, they will awaken in us a greater sense of our own aliveness, because Christ is the Light and that light is the life of man. To truly live in the light will awaken the truth of life in us!

Those who seek God's light will allow it to shine brightly from within, for Christ will live in them and they will live in Christ.

The Mysteries of Light promise so much to those who earnestly seek to contemplate Christ's face through the intercession of Mary's prayer

Approaching the Mysteries

Let us approach the mysteries with a sense of awe and wonder, hoping that Christ in all his fullness will be revealed to us and reveal to us his heart of love.

See Christ's light shining and ask the Holy Spirit to guide you in prayer, that your prayer will truly be heard and answered. Pray that the Holy Spirit will show you how to use each mystery. Ask for a specific focus to hold each person or intention you are praying about, in the centre of each mystery.

An example

Your intention might be to pray for healing for someone. Let Christ's light illuminate the mystery you are praying, and show you an image. Whatever is revealed to you, and it could be different each time – because God shows you many levels of truth – ask yourself: 'What does this say to me? What spiritual truth is being revealed that will bless this prayer?'

What if in the first Mystery of Light, Jesus' Baptism in the Jordan, you are given a picture of sparkling water? What could it mean? It might suggest cleansing, or new life. A vision of the person being 'showered' with the Holy Spirit, washing away all their pain, all hurt, or a vision of the person drinking deeply of the waters of life that flow from Jesus, might emerge to bless your prayer.

Hold this picture in your mind and place the person you are praying for right in the centre of the image. Informed by the scene, pray for the person. In this case we might ask for cleansing by the Holy Spirit, or for the person to be refreshed by Jesus.

This is real, it is not an imagination. It is truth. You are holding the other in truth, and your prayer, surrounded by the power and protection of the Rosary, lifted into the heart of Love, and offered through the intercession of Mary, will surely touch the person on some level. Let Christ's light always be your guide in praying the Mysteries of Light:

Christ's light

↓

illuminating each mystery

↕

giving a focus for prayer

↕

holding the person or situation in the centre of that which is illuminated

↕

surrounded by the power and protection of the Rosary and held in the Heart of Love.

Figure 1: Praying the Mysteries of Light

We see that in praying the Mysteries of Light, the most glorious thing happens – because not only is the person being prayed for touched by Light, but all are blessed and are held in a moment of beauty and truth, beyond space and time. Light then lives more fully in us as a result of each prayer for another.

Exploring the Mysteries

The five Mysteries of Light are concerned with Jesus' ministry on Earth. Jesus brought a new order, a new way of looking at things, of doing things; a new relationship with God. He brought the way of love, forgiveness, redemption and mercy, as the way back to the Father, as the way to find healing and wholeness. He brought a more intimate, familial relationship, which was not in the world previously. He gave himself wholly to us. We receive him into ourselves so that we, too, can be in oneness with God.

By praying each Mystery of Light we touch some special aspect of Jesus' ministry. Through each of the mysteries Jesus is revealing something mystical, not seen or known in this way before his incarnation: the new wineskin, the new order. Through praying and contemplating the mysteries, the Word is brought to light on two levels:

- What Jesus was showing all of us through his actual action/ministry (then)
- What is being revealed to each of us for our own personal insight (now)

Then can be used to illuminate *now*.

The Mysteries of Light can be used as a prayer for another or as the basis for healing prayer for ourselves. Christ's light reveals our true nature and being.

His light shines so brightly and radically that there is no room for illusion or untruth, only what is true is seen. Perhaps you might not feel that good about yourself; you can even believe that you are bad. Through his light, however, you come to see that these negative feelings come from being hurt on some level. On this basis you have built a raft of false thoughts and beliefs about yourself. But in light you begin to see how these are not the truth, just a story you tell yourself.

The light shines inside you and all that is false, all that is not true, is dispelled by the light. Ultimately, the Mysteries of Light are about healing: Christ's light reveals the inner truth, the inner beauty, the inner loveliness of God reflected in us.

Paul was blinded by the light and the light transfigured and transformed him completely. Sometimes we have a long way to travel and can only accept the light in tiny pieces; we all have our own way that is right for us, to receive God's light. Some people have dramatic conversions and with others it is more slow and gentle.

Remember that the Light always reveals God's Holy Truth.

x Is this necessarily so? You can simply have decided to be as you are. Otherwise life is just mechanical puppetry

Encouragement to Go Forward

These mysteries are indeed a treasure – a wonderful gift from God to help us pray; illuminating further the truth and beauty present within all the mysteries of the Rosary.

Let us then ask God, with great confidence and trust, to truly pray these mysteries in accordance with his will. Then let us eagerly pray them, trusting, believing and expecting miracles to happen.

As we pray each mystery we will grow in Christ's Light. Each mystery will bring us closer to seeing the face of Christ and a more intimate knowledge of our Lord. Each mystery builds upon the next, although each can stand alone. There is a flow of Light, which grows and builds as we pray and enter into the Mysteries of Light. The flow, once started, goes forth – increasing in abundance and carrying us further and further into light:

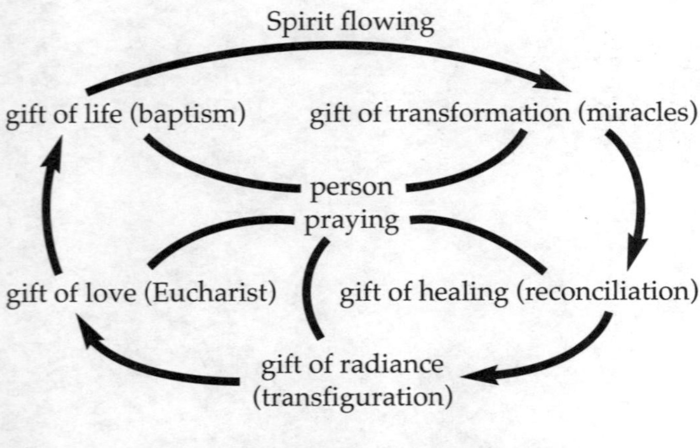

Figure 2: Gifts of the Mysteries of Light

There are indeed many gifts awaiting those willing to embrace the Mysteries of Light. As you begin to pray, so you will be filled with light. As you are filled with light, so you will be filled with the Spirit. As you are filled with the Spirit, you will begin to manifest the fruits and gifts of the Spirit. We will indeed bear much fruit. These gifts can be known by their resonance with love and will always give glory to God.

These additional mysteries are a true gift of love, inspired by the Holy Spirit and brought into being through the wisdom of the Holy Father. It is a momentous event of extraordinary magnitude, from which countless blessings flow.

Those who pray the Mysteries of Light will shine like the stars. Their lives will be beacons of light and peace, shining so all the world can see and know the beauty and truth, the joy and wonder of God with us.

x Mechanical process?

The First Mystery of Light – The Baptism of Jesus in the Jordan

> he . . . came up from the water, and suddenly the heavens opened and he saw the Spirit of God descending like a dove. *Matthew 3:16*

First, let us ask ourselves the question: Where is the light shining? What mystery is being illuminated here? It is the Trinity. What is God saying to each of us? Let us listen. What does it tell us about the mystery of Love? Let us meditate on this.

The first Mystery of Light helps us to see that we are not alone. Jesus is revealed as the Son of God, the Father is heard speaking, and the Spirit is seen as a dove. Here we see Jesus Christ the Light of the world, the Father who is Love, the power of the Holy Spirit; all three together working in unison. This is the Trinity purely and simply illuminated together for the first time. Nothing Jesus does is by himself; it is always with the blessing of the Father and through the power of the Spirit.

From the Trinity, the Holy Spirit flows through us, completely, unpredictably – illuminating what God's Word wants to show us, not what we want to see.

Prayer

Lord God, speak to us this day and help us live our lives to the full; blessed by your Love, flowing in the Power of the Holy Spirit and guided by the Light of your Son. Amen.

X How is all this simple?

xx Where is this said or shown in the baptism?

The Second Mystery of Light – Jesus' Self-manifestation at the Wedding at Cana

The president tasted the water and it had turned into wine. *John 2:9*

Again, let us look for the light. Where does it lead us to in this picture? What is at the centre of our vision? Here we have the occurrence of the first public miracle; the transformation of water into wine. What is the meaning of this miracle? What is Christ's intention? As the Light of the world, what is Christ showing us?

The second mystery lifts us out of narrow vision to the Glory and wonder of God, where miracles can and do happen. Here, then, we can learn that all is not as it seems and that nothing is impossible to God. We see that Transformation is possible for all. There is hope in the darkness. Things can change. We can change – if only we look to God for help.

This mystery shows us that everything has a purpose and that purpose is to illuminate the truth of God's love; everything Jesus did had a meaning and a value. The water becomes wine – a symbol of what is to come at the Passion, as Jesus, filled with the Holy Spirit, becomes the wine, the blood of life for us all. There is much symbolism here referring to the mystery of life as yet to come.

It is not by chance that the water was transformed into wine. The water, used for ablutions, lies unnoticed, contained in humble earthenware jars at the wedding feast. There is a much greater festival yet to come, in which

x These two are not the same

Jesus, the one who was overlooked, will be transformed into the Body and Blood of life.

Jesus' body is an earthenware jar, in the sense that he has taken on our humanity. We, too, as earthenware jars, through God's grace, can hold the mystery of life. We, too, can be transformed into something beautiful and perfect by God's radiance in our lives.

Prayer

Lord – see us, Lord – use us, Lord – transform us with your perfect light. Amen.

x Confusing the vessel with their contents

The Third Mystery of Light – Jesus' Proclamation of the Kingdom of God with His Call to Conversion

> The time is fulfilled, and the kingdom of God is close at hand. Repent, and believe in the gospel. *Mark 1:15*

In the third Mystery of Light we learn to forgive not just each other but ourselves – and even God sometimes – and to be reconciled with Love and ultimately to find Mercy. We learn that the kingdom is here with us now – for we are God's kingdom!

This mystery shines light on our hurts and shows us that the way of healing, the way to life, is through repentance, forgiveness, love and mercy – they are inseparable.

The call to repent frees us from the past, from the ties that bind us in fear, in negativity, that keep us in separation from each other and from God.

Forgiveness is at the centre of Jesus' ministry, as revealed through this mystery. As we forgive, we find freedom and Christ's light shines brighter in us.

Only in forgiveness are we free to love. Jesus' commandment is to love one another as he has loved us; this is how love lives in us and in the world. One with him and his kingdom, we carry his light out into the world, bringing a message of hope.

God's love is absolute, and through his mercy we are forgiven even before we know it. In receiving forgiveness we know we are loved. Reconciliation brings us back to

God, to a state of love where God can live in us and we in him.

Through his act of love Christ reconciled us with the Father; his life is a total gift of reconciliation and love.

This is the meaning of mercy.

Prayer

Help us to be merciful as you are merciful, Lord;
not just with each other, but also with ourselves.
Amen.

The Fourth Mystery of Light – The Transfiguration of Jesus

> There in their presence he was transfigured: his face shone like the sun and his clothes became as dazzling as light. *Matthew 17:3*

The Transfiguration – this is where we see beyond any doubt the truth that Jesus is the Son of God and the Light of the world. In him there is no darkness. His purity shines out.

In this fourth mystery Christ is transfigured. His radiant self is illuminated and his light touches and inspires us. This is the revelation of light *par excellence*. It shows us that we do not have to be overwhelmed or defeated, for Truth is pure and shines brightly; nothing is brighter.

What is incredible is realising that Christ lives in us, and that very same light that was revealed on the mountain is in us too! What a revelation. So how can we feel small and helpless?

Christ is the Light of the world. His true radiance is unmasked. His glory is unveiled. His true beauty is revealed and the Father's voice is heard, echoing the Baptism. The Father says: 'Listen to my Son.'

By listening to the Son, through the power of the Holy Spirit, we will hear the Father more clearly.

For they are inseparable.

Prayer

Lord, may your light touch us, may we embrace it and shine for you – as a beacon of your love for all to see. Amen.

x How can we not?

The Fifth Mystery of Light – Jesus' Institution of the Eucharist at the Last Supper

'Take it and eat,' he said, 'this is my body.' *Matthew 26:26*

The fifth mystery brings us to the Eucharist. The light in this mystery, and indeed in our lives, is Christ, the Light of life, the Life which comes to us in bread and wine.

Through the Holy Eucharist we are given sustenance. Christ's body already revealed to us as Light is now received fully into us, enabling us to shine God's Light in the world. The blessing of the Trinity upon mankind is fulfilled.

Here Christ is revealed in his true glory, both physical and spiritual, through the power of the Holy Spirit – the link between man and God for all time.

Christ himself feeds us. What a glorious blessing. Thus he lives in us intimately and infinitely. As we continue to receive him, and to grow in our awareness of him in us, so we can live our whole lives more fully in him. We come to know him. The blessing of the Trinity upon mankind is fulfilled in him.

As we focus our attention on the Eucharist, his Light reveals his true presence for us.

Through contemplation and love we grow in Christ's Light and begin to shine for him. He shines in us and we live in him.

Because of his gift of life to us through the love of the Father and the power of the Holy Spirit, we are all made one in him.

He sustains and strengthens us and we grow in radiance as we grow in him, through the love of the Father and the power of the Holy Spirit.

Praise be to God.

Alleluia.

Prayer

Lord,

May we grow in awareness of the truth within us as we receive your Holy Eucharist – a promise of Light with us.

Shining Light on the Whole Rosary

Reflecting on the New Mysteries of Light brings us a chance to reconsider the whole Rosary.

Approaching each mystery with faith, confidence and trust, let us ask God to illuminate the abundance of love here present. Let us ask God to enliven our prayer and renew our spirits as we pray.

The Prayers of the Rosary

The Rosary carries us into the very heart of love. Through the intercession and prayers of Mary we are lifted into that place where all things are possible and all is healed and all is made whole. Evil cannot triumph, for love is the victor.

Mary's prayers are at the heart of the Rosary, and Mary's heart is linked to the heart of Jesus, so every prayer brings us directly into contact with both the Immaculate Heart and the Sacred Heart. The prayers of Mary will always be heard by the Son and through the Son will always be heard by the Father, carried by the Holy Spirit – the messenger of Light.

Each prayer of the Rosary has a particular importance. The Rosary begins with the Creed, an affirmation of our faith and our belief, followed by the Our Father, which reminds us that everything that Jesus does leads to the Father, a promise of freedom from the tyranny of evil leading in a natural progression to the Glory Be – the ultimate acknowledgement that all will be well.

x See p 45

These prayers all precede the Hail Mary which leads us to say with Mary: 'Yes'. We accept Christ into our lives and we ask that Mary prays with us. Praying the Rosary we enter more fully into the fulfilment of God's promise, for this prayer, says the Pope, contains 'the *depth of the Gospel message in its entirety*, of which it can be said to be a compendium'.

No wonder the Rosary is such a powerful prayer. The joy, the light, the sorrow and the glory, are all necessary for the healing of the world. The Holy Spirit blesses us through praying these mysteries, flows with us, and lifts us into the mystical and the mystery, uplifting our souls, bringing oneness and wonder, joy and deliverance, and the deepest peace and healing – revealing God's glory for ever and ever.

And so we come to the Joyful, the Sorrowful and the Glorious Mysteries with new light in our hearts and minds. We pray with Mary, the mother of God, in the Power of the Spirit, trusting that we and those we pray for will be lifted further still into the heart of love where miracles happen and joy is complete.

As we look toward Christ's shining face, our relationship with him always at the centre of our prayer, we ask that we will be shown that which we need to see in order that our prayers will be perfectly aligned with his will.

The Joyful Mysteries

Overview

The Joyful Mysteries illuminate the joy and wonder of Jesus Christ come into the world to serve, to love, to be with us.

The light shines on the love, on the peace, on the truth, on the humility of God-with-us. The focus is always on making a choice to love and serve God, whatever the human price. The blessings of God are greater still and incomparable to the cost.

The Joyful Mysteries lead us towards the Mysteries of Light where Jesus' ministry is fulfilled. The Mysteries of Light flow between the Joyful and the Sorrowful Mysteries, lifting us into the fullness of Christ's healing ministry, enabling us to experience more fully the prayer of the Rosary and the power of transformation.

Because the Rosary transcends space and time, what is happening in the Gospel is present to us now.

The Joyful Mysteries are the joy of God-with-us. Joy from heaven blesses all the earth. Joy from God is a perfect spiritual gift, beyond the ordinariness of earthly things.

With Mary's 'yes' nothing can be the same again. For God is with us in a new way and he is love: the love that heals, restores, forgives all – joy indeed.

The Joyful Mysteries inspire us, then, to come to God, to open our hearts and say 'yes'. To serve God. Let us approach them now as children of God.

The First Joyful Mystery: The Annunciation

> You see before you the Lord's servant, let it happen to me as you have said. *Luke 1:38*

Experience here the joy of following God's perfect will, of saying 'yes', of being caught up in the greatest of all mysteries: the love of God. Mary's joy comes from her total acceptance of God's will. It is an act of pure faith, trust and steadfast humility, to let God's will be done with no questioning, no fear, no preoccupation with worldly things. Mary fully accepts the Word of God, the Light of the world, into her whole being. To hear God's message and to accept it with joy, what more could we hope for? What a perfect moment, leading to the reconciliation of all, for all time.

The light in this mystery, shining in Mary's heart, is made to shine in ours. Praise God indeed.

The Second Joyful Mystery: The Visitation

> The child leapt in her womb and Elizabeth was filled with the Holy Spirit. She gave a loud cry and said, 'Of all women you are the most blessed, and blessed is the fruit of your womb.' *Luke 1:41-43*

Mary is the bearer of light, and even though she carries within her the most precious gift in earth and heaven, still she humbly offers her services in love to Elizabeth who is also with child. The Holy Spirit illuminates the truth of Mary carrying Jesus, the Son of God, within her.

Mary comes to serve Elizabeth – and joy is revealed.

John the Baptist will be the one who announces Christ's presence and ministry to the people. So great is John spiritually, and so sensitive is he to the Christ Light, that he leaps for joy in his mother's womb. No wonder he will be the one to prepare the way for the saviour. He is so utterly filled with the Holy Spirit that his whole being has to acknowledge Christ's presence in the world: a recognition of what is yet to come. May we, too, be blessed with the sensitivity to recognise Christ's presence in our lives, in all the secret places.

The Third Joyful Mystery: The Birth of Jesus

> Today in the town of David a Saviour has been born to you; he is Christ the Lord. And here is a sign for you: you will find a baby wrapped in swaddling clothes and lying in a manger. *Luke 2: 9-12*

How can we describe the joy of Jesus being born? The light of the world has come into the world and is reflected in the radiance of the star, illuminating the joy of heaven and the song of angels, praising God in all his vulnerability, humility, tenderness. The hope of the world come to serve and to do the will of God is found in simplicity – lying in a manger, surrounded by oxen and an ass.

His beauty shines anew for us all – may our hearts be tenderly opened to love. Let us listen in the stillness, as the shepherds did, to hear the songs of heaven and rejoice at the coming of God into our lives. Let joy flood our being and bless our daily lives. Let us sing songs of praise and thanks for new life, for God's light.

The Fourth Joyful Mystery: The Presentation in the Temple

> My eyes have seen the salvation which you have made ready in the sight of the nations; a light of revelation for the gentiles and glory for your people Israel. *Luke 2:30-32*

Here is the Son being brought before his heavenly Father, an affirmation of the path that lies ahead, and a confirmation of Mary's 'yes'. The light of the world shines brightly now; lighting the path of hope for all time.

This is indeed a joyful moment.

For Anna and Simeon it is the supreme confirmation; it is everything they have ever asked for. Filled with the Holy Spirit, they know the truth that God has come into the world and his promise is fulfilled. What blessings, what joy, abounds for those who have eyes to see. What hope the light of the world carries for all mankind.

May we, too, lift our hearts and all for whom we pray into the light, for our Heavenly Father's blessing.

The Fifth Joyful Mystery: The Finding of the Child Jesus in the Temple

> Three days later, they found him in the Temple, sitting among the teachers, listening to them, and asking them questions. *Luke 2:46*

Mary's love for her son is mixed with her earthly fears and anxieties. Jesus is lost for three days from his mother – a sign of the path ahead for them both, for Jesus will be 'lost' for three days on his Father's business, from his death on the Cross till his resurrection three days later.

Jesus is always in intimate relationship with the Father, always serving him perfectly. This is a lesson of love and trust.

The light shines clearly on the truth that Jesus is the Word of God.

May we also listen to and be taught by the Word of God – may we learn to trust that, even if he seems lost to us, God is working in and through Christ, to bring us to a place of trust and love.

The Sorrowful Mysteries

Overview

As we contemplate Christ's passion and enter into the pain and grief of a hurting world, so we cannot fail to open our hearts to the needs and pain of others. We cannot fail to be touched by the deep sorrow of these mysteries and come to feel God's grief for his children.

We must not approach the Cross with fear and trepidation. No, we need to approach it with humility and tenderness. An absolute and complete healing love deserves our fullest attention, that the wisdom and truth of the Cross may begin to be illuminated in our hearts. For this is the ultimate place of healing and hope for all mankind, for all time.

In the Sorrowful Mysteries, we look through the tears and prayers of Mary, to the Light which brings hope and transformation. We do not get overwhelmed by grief or fear or despair. Always at the centre of the Sorrowful Mysteries is Christ, whose light is greater than any shadow, any agony or darkness, reuniting us all to the Father.

If you truly pray these mysteries and touch the love of Christ, you will embrace his deepest sorrow and cry the healing tears of love; a gift of the Holy Spirit for the whole world.

The First Sorrowful Mystery: The Agony in the Garden

> 'Father,' he said, 'if you are willing, take this cup away from me. Nevertheless, let your will be done, not mine.' Then an angel appeared to him, coming from heaven to give him strength. *Luke 22:42-45*

Here Jesus is abandoned even by his closest friends. However, the angels minister to him and he is in communion with the Father. His grief is immense and his sorrow such that he sweats tears of blood. There is the echo of Mary's yes from the Joyful Mysteries, in that Christ chooses the will of the Father – he says: 'Your will be done.' He would rather not do what is asked of him by God, but he does what the Father asks of him, because God's will is made perfect in love. Whatever action we do, if aligned with God's will, it will become a perfect act of love.

The Second Sorrowful Mystery: The Scourging at the Pillar

> Pilate then had Jesus taken away and scourged. *John 19:1*

We see Christ stripped of his clothes; he is naked and exposed to all sorts of abuse, torment, violence, pain, humiliation and, again, earthly abandonment. What we have to look to, is the act of love. Looking at the pain of the scourging, Christ illuminates his love by taking on pain, by holding and experiencing all those things that wound and damage; and being love in response. He is not fighting back, or being abusive, judging, angry, rebellious – as we might be. He is taking on all the hurts and holding them in his love. He is just being there with that and sometimes we just have to be there with that too. The light teaches us how to hold pain in love.

The Third Sorrowful Mystery: The Crowning of Thorns

> The soldiers twisted some thorns into a crown and put it on his head, and dressed him in a purple robe. They kept coming up to him and saying, 'Hail, king of the Jews!' and slapping him in the face. *John 19:1-3*

Each thorn pierces Christ's flesh and mingles with his blood. His blood is the life of the world, so he is experiencing every hurt intimately and infinitely. This echoes the sweating of the blood in the garden; they are like tears of blood, each drop of blood a tear of life, representing the deep wounding of souls, so that all are known intimately by Christ himself. Our pain, the world's pain, is intricately mingled with Christ's blood; he is suffering with us and knows the depth of sin in the world and is there with us in all our pain and even terror. That is what the light shows us; that we are not alone, that every agony is known and touched and held in the heart of love and is marked on Christ's body.

The Fourth Sorrowful Mystery: The Carrying of the Cross

> They led him out to crucify him. They enlisted a passer-by, Simon of Cyrene, father of Alexander and Rufus, who was coming in from the country, to carry his cross.
> *Mark 15:21-22*

Jesus is carrying the weight of suffering of the world. The cross is so heavy; the suffering, wrongdoing, sin, the absence of love in the world, our separation from God, is so great. He is so weak from the torture, punishment and pain already experienced, that it is almost overwhelming and he stumbles and falls from the weight. There is so much grief and pain and hate in the world.

But then he is helped to carry the cross by Simon. Christ needs us in the world to carry and support the pain of the world with him: 'I am the vine, you are the branches.' There is a mystical union and a desire and a need for unity or communion in the world that is represented by Simon, who gives his strength to help Jesus.

Perhaps Simon also represents the poverty of our own pain and the naked vulnerability of walking with Christ. There is a stripping away of worldly vanity and pride, of fears and embarrassments, when we get close to carrying the pain of the world. The light in this mystery is the light of compassion and the vulnerability and nakedness of God's love and need for us.

The Fifth Sorrowful Mystery: The Crucifixion

> But Jesus, again crying out in a loud voice, yielded up his spirit. *Matthew 27:50*

The crucifixion brings us to the heart of love. The greatest sorrow leads on to the greatest glory. We must not get stuck in the utter desolation and desperation of death, but see the choice that Christ makes on the Cross to embrace all in the mystery of life.

As his arms are outstretched, he embraces the whole world. His heart is truly opened, his love is complete. His choice is to do the will of God, which is love and mercy. All is healed in an act of pure love, all is embraced and touched so that sin and evil can hold no power over us, for the love of God is greater still. As Jesus embraces us all and holds us tenderly and lovingly, so too does the Father hold the Son and thus the mission of love given by God the Father is complete.

Even the dead, even those furthest away from God's light, are embraced, and a path of light opens up, leading back to oneness. This is the truth of the Cross. Jesus dies but he is the one who holds death. Death cannot hold him, for he is greater still, held in the love of the Trinity, bringing healing for all time.

All the joy, the sorrow, the pain and all the tears, come together on the Cross and are transformed and healed by the Light of the world, who holds and blesses them and brings life. Glory be to God.

We must not be too afraid to look into the heart of pain, because that is where we find the gift – the gift of healing, of rebirth, of life, of hope.

We have to remember that even if we do not see the Father, he is there and nothing is wasted, nothing is impossible to God.

Travelling along the path of Christ's passion with him may seem like a dark road, may cause us to avert our eyes, to even run away, as Peter did. Yet if we go forward in love, we begin to see and know the miracle of Christ's gift of life to us. We see beyond death to the witness and fullness of God's love now revealed in the Glorious Mysteries.

The Glorious Mysteries

Overview

And so it is that the Glorious Mysteries complete the circle of love, bringing us into a place of oneness and service to God, lifting us into the knowledge that all things are possible when viewed with the eyes of love and the power of the Holy Spirit.

The Glorious Mysteries light up the truth of Christ's mission on earth – they reveal the glory of God absolutely. Nothing is impossible to God, all is made whole and well in the purity and truth of his love – even death cannot hold him. God is Life and God is Light and God is Love – and, what is most incredible, he gives that life, that light, that love to us.

Glory be to God indeed.

The First Glorious Mystery: The Resurrection

> Why look among the dead for someone who is alive? He is not here; he has risen. *Luke 24:6*

How does God light up his glory for us to see? Let us look beyond the possible. Let us look beyond the visible. Let us look with spiritual eyes to see the spiritual mystery and glory of God revealed.

The tomb where Jesus body lay is empty, despite a guard being present at all times. The stone has been rolled away. God is not here in the emptiness of death – no – he is risen. Love has brought him back to life.

Only God, through faith and prayer, can help us glimpse some understanding of the power of this love.

With this new vision, then, all things, all needs, all wants, all hurts, all purpose, can be transformed from seeming loss and emptiness into the wonder and glory of new life.

Nothing can be the same any more – for Christ has died and Christ is risen and he has held us all in his heart and so nothing can be lost or wasted or destroyed when we touch this truth – when we trust in Jesus, who is mercy, who is love, who is God. This is the amazing truth of Easter Day – transformation, hope, joy, love – nothing can ever be the same again when we see the risen Christ in all his glory.

As we pray this mystery then, let us ask for that vision of truth and there hold all that we pray for. How can our prayer not be answered? This is the power of love revealed on this holy morning.

The Second Glorious Mystery: The Ascension

> Raising his hands he blessed them. Now as he blessed them, he withdrew from them and was carried up to heaven. *Luke 24:50-51*

What do we see when we contemplate Jesus ascending into heaven? What glorious mystery is unfolding before our eyes? It is the mystery of the body of Christ, now immanent, transcending into heaven to be with the Father, lifting us all with him – our humanity carried with him, so that we, too, may live in the love of the Father and the Son. This is the promise of the ascension – yet to be manifest when the Holy Spirit comes; and we shall be disciples too – we shall bear witness to Christ and he shall be with us to the end of time. What an incredible promise, a promise of life – all glory to God.

The Third Glorious Mystery: The Coming of the Holy Spirit

> They were all filled with the Holy Spirit, and began to speak different languages as the Spirit gave them power to express themselves. *Acts 2:1-5*

The light shines by the power of God coming down from heaven, bringing freedom on every level: freedom to speak, preach, heal. God's glory is illuminated for all to see. Jesus' death and resurrection are fulfilled with the coming of the Holy Spirit, transforming all in its path, for it is only when the Spirit comes that Christ's mission is complete. It is only with the Spirit that we can clearly see the power of God working in our lives and we can know it is the Spirit because the Spirit brings glory to God. So it is with the coming of the Spirit that the gifts and fruits of the Spirit are made manifest, that we might serve God in the world.

When the Spirit comes, there is joy, freedom, hope, healing, transformation – and nothing is the same again. Miracles happen and God's promise is complete, and so we say, 'Come, Holy Spirit, come, shine your light in our hearts and transform us so that we might be perfect instruments for the glory of God.'

The Fourth Glorious Mystery: The Assumption

> And how could a thing subsist had you not willed it? Or how be preserved if not called forth by you? . . . For your imperishable spirit is in everything! *Wisdom 11:25; 12:1*

The Assumption is the completion of Mary's earthly mission and the beginning of her heavenly one. It is the completion of Mary's 'yes' from the Annunciation. It is a blessing and glory of God because of the humility and total acceptance of the Light of the world into her whole being. It is the triumphant passage of life beloved into the heart of love. It is the blessing of humanity.

The light is focusing not on the end of a life, but on the beginning of the true life held in God. It is the beginning of joy unending and even greater service still, because Mary becomes the Mother of the Church in heaven, through the will of God and the power of the Holy Spirit and the love of the Son. The light shines on the awe and wonder of God's greatness and the life yet to come for us all, if only we can say 'yes'.

The Fifth Glorious Mystery: The Crowning of Mary, Queen of Heaven

> Now a great sign appeared in heaven: a woman, robed with the sun, standing on the moon, and on her head a crown of twelve stars. *Revelation 12:1*

All glory is given to God, though the humility and service of a pure heart on earth now crowned in glory; through Mary's acceptance to bear the Son of God and to bear the pain alongside her Son. She has shared and born witness to the suffering and the healing of the world and all mankind through her goodness and love. Evil has been vanquished through the simplicity of her acceptance of love. Mary's role has been intimately linked to the healing and saving love of her Son. She is blessed most high in heaven for this service and her prayers always reflect the Light of the world.

How can God refuse her prayers and so we can know with all trust and faith that a prayer asked of the Virgin Mary in heaven will always be answered because of the love and intimacy between the Trinity and herself.

It is not Mary who answers the prayers of the faithful, but Mary offers our petition in love and compassion to the Son. The light of Mary will always shine on the Son, the light of the Son will always bless the Mother of God, for victory is complete, all evil is vanquished and God's light shines triumphant in the world. All glory and honour to God. Amen.

Mary's light will always guide us to the Son. She is all humility, all goodness, all worshipful – she acts as a sign in heaven, always pointing to the Christ.

And so it is that the glorious mysteries complete the circle of love, bringing us into a place of oneness and service to God, lifting us into the knowledge that all things are possible when viewed with the eyes of love and the power of the Holy Spirit.

Pope John Paul II's Suggestions for Enriching Your Prayer of the Rosary

In his address of 16 October 2002, *Rosarium Virginis Mariae,** John Paul II made certain suggestions to enrich and enhance how we pray the rosary.

He suggests that we perhaps use an icon to set the scene and to prepare for prayer. An icon is a means of moving from the physical to the spiritual, just as Christ took on bodily form, in order to lead us to the divine.

As each mystery is announced, follow it with a related scripture passage. Depending on the circumstances, this can be a long or short passage. As we listen to the inspired Word, Pope John Paul says that we can be sure that 'this is the word of God, spoken for today and spoken "for me" '. How reassuring to know that God is speaking to each of us in a personal and special way.

The Pope places great emphasis on silence – for it nourishes our meditation – and it is so difficult to achieve these days. It is in the silence that we can most clearly hear God speak.

After the announcement and proclamation of the Word, he suggests that we pause and silently focus our attention on the mystery to come, before moving into vocal prayer. This increases our awareness of God's presence and the message that he has for us.

---

* Apostolic Letter of the Supreme Pontiff John Paul II to the Bishops, Clergy and Faithful, *Rosarium Virginis Mariae,* on the Most Holy Rosary, 16 October 2002

Everything Jesus does leads to the Father. That is why the first prayer of the Rosary is the Lord's Prayer. Through Jesus' relationship with the Father and with us, we are gathered together as brothers and sisters, as Church, for this profound meditation.

When praying the ten Hail Marys, it is important to remember that the most important part of the Hail Mary, the 'centre of gravity', is the name of Jesus. The Pope praises the custom of highlighting the name of Christ by adding a clause referring to the mystery being contemplated.

So we could pray, for example:

'Hail Mary, full of grace, the Lord is with thee, blessed art thou among women and blessed is the fruit of thy womb, Jesus . . .'

- *carried in humility by the Virgin Mary*
- *recognised by John the Baptist even in his mother's womb*
- *the Light of the world, born for us on earth*
- *presented in the Temple to his Heavenly Father*
- *on his Father's business*
- *baptised by the Holy Spirit*
- *miraculously transforming water into wine*
- *whose heart is mercy*
- *transfigured on the mountain*
- *the Bread of Life*
- *ministered to by angels*
- *scourged at the pillar*
- *crowned with thorns*
- *carrying the Cross*
- *crucified for us*

- *risen from the dead*
- *ascended into heaven*
- *speaking through the Holy Spirit*
- *who received his mother's body and soul into heaven*
- *who honours his mother as Queen of Heaven*

. . . Holy Mary, Mother of God, pray for us sinners, now and at the hour of our death. Amen.

The Glory Be raises our minds to the heights of heaven. It must be given due prominence, the Pope points out, ideally by being sung, especially during public recital of the Rosary.

Make an effort, says the Holy Father, to end each mystery with a prayer for the fruits 'specific to that particular mystery'. It is a challenge, yet in this way the Rosary is made more meaningful for the everyday Christian life. The prayer itself can take on a variety of forms specific to different spiritual traditions and Christian communities.

After the mysteries have been prayed, it is only natural, says the Pope, for the soul to want to burst forth in a prayer of praise, for example, praying the Hail Holy Queen, or a prayer such as the Salve Regina to Mary, the beloved Mother of God's Son, our teacher and our guide.

Finally, the Rosary should end with a prayer for the Pope, for in this way our vision and prayer is expanded to embrace all the needs of the Church.

Let us remember that this is 'the crowning moment of an inner journey which has brought the faithful into living contact with the mystery of Christ and his Blessed Mother'.

No wonder the Pope asks us to renew our dedication to the Rosary, to this most powerful form of prayer. Praise and thanks be to God.

Appendix

How to Pray the Rosary

'Paternoster Row' in London owes its name to the earliest form of the Rosary, the *Pater noster*, from the Latin for the opening words of the Lord's Prayer; a set of beads to help the laity who mostly could not read, to keep count while they recited 150 Our Fathers, in lieu of the 150 psalms, the Psalter, prayed by the monks.

Later, the practice grew of reciting 150 Hail Marys, and the beads became known as the 'Rosary' – after the rose. This very precious prayer, then, was brought to the Church by ordinary people out of their desire to pray and meditate upon the life of Christ.

The Rosary has been called the 'Little Gospel' because of the way the original fifteen mysteries – and now also the Mysteries of Light – present a digest of the Gospel. This highlights a very important element of the Rosary, again inspired by the great monastic orders, the *Lectio Divina* or Holy Reading, with the distinct advantage that no books or literacy skills are required, simply a pair of beads or even just ten fingers (or toes).

Praying the Rosary is easy, for it is designed to lead you into prayer. Imagine a friend showing you around their rose garden. First you would have to approach the garden. Then, as you stroll around, your friend might well proudly announce each species of rose. Stooping, you gently caress each exquisite bloom, touching the petals, drinking in the heavenly perfume. 'Glory to God!' you might exclaim at such wondrous beauty.

Similarly, let the beads lead you to a heavenly bouquet. We begin with a blessing. Make the Sign of the Cross,

x Why? Mystic Rose?

saying, 'In the name of the Father, and of the Son, and of the Holy Spirit. Amen.'

Taking hold of the cross on your beads, begin to pray:

The Apostles' Creed

I believe in God, the Father Almighty,
Creator of Heaven and earth.
I believe in Jesus Christ, his only Son, our Lord.
He was conceived by the power of the Holy Spirit and was born of the Virgin Mary.
He suffered under Pontius Pilate,
was crucified, died, and was buried.
He descended to the dead.
On the third day he rose again.
He ascended into heaven,
and is seated at the right hand of the Father.
He will come again to judge the living and the dead.
I believe in the Holy Spirit,
the Holy Catholic Church,
the Communion of Saints,
the forgiveness of sins,
the resurrection of the body,
and life everlasting. Amen.

The first bead that follows the cross is for praying the Our Father.

Our Father

Our Father, who art in heaven,
hallowed be thy name.
Thy kingdom come,
thy will be done, on earth as it is in heaven.
Give us this day our daily bread,

and forgive us our trespasses,
as we forgive those who trespass against us,
and lead us not into temptation;
but deliver us from evil. Amen.

Next, the group of three beads are for three Hail Marys, which traditionally are prayed for the three theological virtues of Faith, Hope and Charity.

Hail Mary

Hail Mary, full of grace, the Lord is with thee.
Blessed art thou among women, and blessed is the fruit of thy womb, Jesus.
Holy Mary, mother of God, pray for us sinners
now and at the hour of our death. Amen.

On the final bead of this string, and the first bead of the rest of the rosary, we offer praise to God :

Glory Be

Glory be to the Father, and to the Son, and to the Holy Spirit,
as it was in the beginning, is now, and ever shall be, world without end. Amen.

You have now arrived at the beginning of the main body of beads, this garland of roses, ready for your journey into the heart of love.

The first mystery is announced. On a Monday it will be the Joyful Mysteries that you pray, on Tuesdays the Sorrowful, on Wednesdays the Glorious, on Thursdays the Mysteries of Light, on Fridays the Sorrowful Mysteries, on Saturday the Joyful and on Sunday the Glorious Mysteries.

You will notice that there are five groups of ten beads, each separated by a single bead. The single bead is for praying the Our Father at the beginning of each mystery and the Glory Be at the end. The beads in between are for praying the ten Hail Marys, called a decade.

So the pattern is this:

- Announce each mystery
- Pray the Our Father
- Pray the ten Hail Marys
- Pray the Glory Be

In between each decade we are greatly encouraged to insert an appropriate prayer, as we explore below. A much-loved prayer, requested by Mary at Fatima on 13 June 1917, is:

O my Jesus, forgive us our sins,
save us from the fires of hell,
and lead all souls to heaven,
especially those in most need of your mercy. Amen.

Finally, at the end of the fifth mystery, and if your rosary has one attached, you will arrive at the medal. On this you are invited to pray, after the last Glory Be:

Hail, Holy Queen, Mother of Mercy, hail our life, our sweetness and our hope! To thee do we cry, poor banished children of Eve; to thee do we send up our sighs, mourning and weeping in this valley of tears. Turn then, most gracious advocate, thine eyes of mercy toward us, and after this our exile, show unto us the blessed fruit of thy womb, Jesus. O clement, O loving, O sweet Virgin Mary!

V. Pray for us, O Holy Mother of God.

R. That we may be made worthy of the promises of Christ.

This is often followed by:

Let us pray. O God, whose only begotten Son, by his life, death and resurrection, has purchased for us the rewards of eternal life, grant, we beseech thee, that meditating upon these mysteries of the most holy Rosary of the Blessed Virgin Mary, we may imitate what they contain and obtain what they promise, through the same Christ Our Lord. Amen.